100

THINGS TO DO IN
THE NORTH
GEORGIA MOUNTAINS
BEFORE YOU
DIE

AJ,

Enjoy your
adventures in the
North Georgia Mountains!.

Karen
Warren

100

THINGS TO DO IN
THE NORTH
GEORGIA MOUNTAINS
BEFORE YOU
DIE

• •

KARON WARREN

REEDY PRESS

Library of Congress Control Number: 2022936987

ISBN: 9781681063904

Design by Jill Halpin

All photos by the author unless otherwise noted.

Printed in the United States of America
22 23 24 25 26   5 4 3 2 1

Photo credit: Len Garrison, Seeing Southern

CONTENTS

● ●

Music and Entertainment

Culture and History

PREFACE

Growing up in Marietta, my family was like thousands of others in the Metro Atlanta area. We routinely visited popular spots in the North Georgia Mountains like Helen, enjoyed the view at the Tallulah Gorge Overlook, and got apples in Ellijay. Every fall, we trekked up to the North Georgia Mountains to see the fall foliage, eat at the Dillard House Restaurant, and stock up on hot-boiled peanuts. It was a favorite family tradition we all looked forward to every year.

Fast-forward to 2001 when I married an Ellijay native and moved to this small North Georgia town. Living in the North Georgia Mountains provided a new perspective. I got to know the people, their businesses, and why they loved this region so much. I started visiting other communities—Blue Ridge, Dahlonega, Cleveland, Hiawassee, Clayton, and others—and discovered these mountain towns had a lot to offer, not just for locals but also visitors.

As a freelance writer, I started telling the stories of the people, the places, and the businesses of the North Georgia Mountains. The more I learned and discovered, the more I realized there was much, much more to learn and discover.

• •

Even with 100 things in this book, it barely scratches the surface of all this region has to offer. But I hope it will be an impetus to starting your own discoveries, your own adventures, in the North Georgia Mountains.

● ●

ACKNOWLEDGMENTS

Thank you to all my writing friends who have been patient with me as I bombarded them with questions about writing a book. Thanks, too, for the many public relations professionals who helped provide information, especially on deadline. A shout-out and thank you to Judy and Len Garrison of Seeing Southern Photography for providing such gorgeous photos. And a special thank-you to my husband and kids for their unwavering support as I tackled this project.

Photo credit: Len Garrison, Seeing Southern

FOOD AND DRINK

GET YOUR FILL OF COUNTRY COOKING
AT THE DILLARD HOUSE

Since 1917 when Carrie and Arthur Dillard invited their first guest to enjoy a meal, the Dillard House restaurant in Dillard has welcomed visitors to dine family style at tables filled with fried chicken, country ham, barbecue ribs, country fried steak, rice, gravy, creamed corn, collard greens, fried okra, black-eyed peas, acorn squash soufflé, coleslaw, and more. Also, don't miss the homemade yeast rolls and cornbread served with the Dillard House's apple butter (take home your own from the gift shop!). Before or after your meal, stroll to the stables to visit the horses, or sit back and relax in one of the many rocking chairs along the front porch. While fall is a popular time to visit, any time of year is the right time for a meal at the Dillard House.

768 Franklin St., Dillard, 706-746-5348
dillardhouse.com

TIP

Wait times can be extremely long on weekends, especially Sundays, so plan accordingly if you don't want to wait. Another not-to-miss family-style restaurant is the Smith House in Dahlonega.

84 S. Chestatee St., Dahlonega
706-725-8148

GRAB YOUR FAVORITE SOUP AND SANDWICH
AT CANTABERRY

With locations in Ellijay and Blue Ridge, Cantaberry offers a variety of homemade soups and sandwiches that quickly earned the restaurant a well-deserved reputation as *the* lunch spot. Two of the signature dishes include the chicken and wild rice soup and the chicken salad made with all-white chicken, mayo, grapes, and candied pecans. Burgers, salads, and sides also are available. In addition, the Ellijay location is open for dinner, with a menu of appetizers, soups, salads, burgers, and specialty entrées like Cantaberry meatloaf, fresh trout, and Southern fried chicken. Finish off any meal with one of the many decadent desserts, such as coconut cake, lemon pound cake, Mississippi mud bars, and lemon bars. Both locations also offer a beer and wine menu.

5 S. Side Square, Ellijay, 706-636-4663

524 E. Main St., Blue Ridge, 706-946-7687

cantaberry.com

ENJOY
YOUR FAVORITE BARBECUE
AT THE PINK PIG

Located in Cherry Log, the Pink Pig serves some of the most popular pit-cooked barbecue in the North Georgia Mountains. Founded by Bud Holloway in 1967, people near and far travel to the Pink Pig for pulled pork, brisket, Brunswick stew, baked beans, and the ever-popular garlic salad. Today, Bud's granddaughter, Samantha, and her husband, Jacob, run the Pink Pig, carrying on Bud's time-honored traditions. In fact, family continues to be a strong theme here, as evidenced by the menu. Try the Sam's Special, a large barbecue pork sandwich on garlic toast with chips and a pickle, or Bubba's Brisket Nachos, beef brisket served over deep-fried chips and covered with cheese. Other family members' namesake dishes appear on the menu as well. Also, don't miss the homemade cobbler or banana pudding.

824 Cherry Log St., Cherry Log, 706-276-3311
pinkpigcherrylog.com

JUMP ON THE BALL GROUND BURGER BUS
FOR A TASTY MEAL

In the heart of downtown Ball Ground, the Ball Ground Burger Bus welcomes diners to enjoy handcrafted burgers using certified Black Angus beef that is all natural, farm-raised, and hormone-free. While the kitchen sits in a brick building, the dining room is in the circa-1948 electric Atlanta Transit Authority trolley #1386 that carried passengers around downtown Atlanta from 1948 until the 1960s. The menu is as eclectic as the dining room. There's the Fried Green Jacket with two fried green tomatoes, pimento cheese, and wasabi ranch atop a patty of the restaurant's fresh ground special blend. Or you can have Dad's on Death Row, with cheddar cheese, fried egg, fried grits, bacon, and maple syrup atop your patty. Less adventurous eaters can create their own burger, or select one of the deep-fried dogs. Regardless of what you choose, this culinary ride won't leave you stranded.

288 Gilmer Ferry Rd., Ball Ground, 678-454-2422
facebook.com/BGBurgerBus

EXPLORE GERMAN CUISINE
AT HOFER'S OF HELEN

For breakfast and lunch, sample some of the best authentic German cuisine at Hofer's of Helen in downtown Helen. Founded by Horst and Gerda Hofer, this bakery, konditorei, and café features favorite dishes from the Hofers' hometown of Schwabach, Germany. For instance, at breakfast you can have apfelkuechle, batter-dipped sliced apples that are grilled, sprinkled with cinnamon sugar, and topped with whipped cream. At lunch, try the Ziguener schnitzel, a lightly breaded and pan-fried pork cutlet topped with a spicy green and red pepper sauce. If you prefer, you can grab something from the bakery for dessert or to have as a sweet treat later. Think hazelnut rum torte, chocolate custard éclair, cream puffs, or apple strudel. This is the perfect place to put you in the Bavarian spirit that the Alpine village of Helen has to offer.

8758 N. Main St., Helen, 706-878-8200
hofers.com

DIG INTO SOUTHERN FAVORITES
AT UNION SOCIAL

At Union Social in Blairsville, choose from a menu of hearty Southern selections that are sure to satisfy any appetite. For instance, start with the Country Caprese, which is fried green tomatoes topped with housemade pimento cheese and tangy chow chow, or chicken waffle sliders complete with buffalo trace bourbon syrup. Then you can move on to the classic meatloaf or chicken biscuit pie, which features a centerpiece of mashed potatoes surrounded by buttermilk biscuits covered with a creamy sauce of roasted chicken breast, peas, carrots, onions, and mushrooms. Of course, you can't leave without a taste of a Southern dessert, so check out the sweet bread pudding: glazed donuts soaked and baked in a sweet custard and dressed in a peach cobbler filling. While dining, you can enjoy live music, bar bingo, and other nightly entertainment.

171 Copperhead Pkwy., Blairsville, 706-745-8000

TIP
When dining with friends and family, Union Social requires parties of eight and larger to make a reservation.

SIP YOUR FAVORITE WINE
AT A NORTH GEORGIA WINERY

More than 40 years ago, vintners discovered the conditions in the North Georgia Mountains were ideal for growing grapes. The combination of the region's elevation, soil, and climate provides an optimal location for producing high-quality wine grapes that are then crafted into some of the best varietals available in the country. In fact, many Georgia wineries boast a wide array of award-winning vintages. They also feature on-site tasting rooms, restaurants, live music events, patios, and more where you can enjoy a glass of your favorite vino. For example, at Cartecay Vineyards in Ellijay, you can take a seat on the Chimney Patio, relax with a glass of red or white, listen to some live music, and take in scenic views of the surrounding vineyard. Spend the afternoon, or include Cartecay Vineyards in a full-day tour of local wineries.

5704 Clear Creek Rd., Ellijay, 706-698-9463
cartecayvineyards.com

TIP

With more than 50 wineries and vineyards in the North Georgia Mountains, it's impossible to list them all here. To find out more about North Georgia wineries and vineyards, visit the Georgia Wine Producers website (georgiawineproducers. org) or the Winegrowers Association of Georgia website (georgiawine.org).

PICK A PECK OF APPLES
AT R&A ORCHARDS

Georgia may be known as the Peach State, but apples reign in the North Georgia Mountains. You'll find the largest concentration of apple houses and orchards in Ellijay, located in the Apple Capital of Georgia (Gilmer County), but you'll also find them in Alto, Blue Ridge, Lakemont, and McCaysville. Visitors show up in droves to pick their own apples during the fall when apples are in season. Although most of the apple houses are open seasonally, R&A Orchards in Ellijay operates year-round. You'll find a variety of fruits and vegetables in the farm market based on what's in season. You also can pick up jellies, jams, salsas, honey, dried apple chips, and other items. The apple house also features its own bakery and café, where you can enjoy chicken and dumplings, fresh fried pies, and, when in season, homemade peach or strawberry ice cream.

5505 Hwy. 52 E., Ellijay, 706-273-3821
randaorchards.com

TIP
Traffic at the apple houses can be insane during the fall, so plan to spend the day in the area and have a lot of patience waiting to get in and out of apple-house parking lots.

OTHER APPLE HOUSES TO VISIT

Aaron Family Orchards
8350 Hwy. 52 E., Ellijay, 706-273-3180/706-273-8456
aaronfamilyorchards.com

BJ Reece Orchards
9131 Hwy. 52 E., Ellijay, 706-276-3048
reeceorchards.com

Deep Roots Orchard
2984 Mobile Rd., McCaysville, 706-492-7753
folkapothic.com

Hillcrest Orchards
9696 Hwy. 52 E., Ellijay, 706-273-3838
hillcrestorchards.net

Hillside Orchard Farms
18 Sorghum Mill Dr., Lakemont, 800-262-9429
hillsideorchard.com

Jaemor Farms
5340 Cornelia Hwy., Alto, 770-869-3999
jaemorfarms.com

Mercier Orchards
8660 Blue Ridge Dr., Blue Ridge, 706-632-3411
mercier-orchards.com

Panorama Orchards & Farm Market
63 Talona Spur, Ellijay , 706-276-3813
panoramaorchards.com

Penland's Apple House
41 Talona Mountain Rd., Ellijay, 706-635-5110
7678 Tails Creek Rd., Ellijay, 706-635-5100
facebook.com/penlandapples

Red Apple Barn
3379 Tails Creek Rd., Ellijay, 706-635-5898
redapplebarn.com

SCREAM FOR ICE CREAM
AT MOOBEARS

When the craving hits for creamy, hand-dipped ice cream, head to MooBears to satisfy your taste buds. Located in Blue Ridge, MooBears offers more than 20 flavors ranging from black cherry to pistachio almond to mint chocolate chip and cookie dough. You'll also find seasonal flavors and flavors of the month that are available for a limited time, so get those quick. For those who don't want to ruin their dinner, MooBears also features a menu of delicious hot dogs. Housed in the Moo'Caboo near the Blue Ridge Scenic Railway, there is outdoor seating if you prefer to eat before strolling through downtown Blue Ridge. Also, keep in mind MooBears is operating on the same schedule as the train, so if the train isn't running, MooBears is not open. As such, check the train schedule before making plans to visit.

678 E. Main St., Blue Ridge, 706-946-2622
moobearsicecream.com
facebook.com/moobearsicecream

TEMPT YOUR
TASTE BUDS AT HARVEST ON MAIN

Touted as "Southern-inspired global cuisine," Harvest on Main serves up a variety of dishes not normally found at North Georgia Mountains restaurants. Think confit of duck with butternut squash ravioli, house bacon, golden raisins, arugula, cream, and smoked gouda. Or tortelloni puttanesca with three cheese-filled pasta, capers, olives, rosemary, tomato, shaved garlic, smoked ricotta, and extra virgin olive oil. But there are dishes that are more in tune with the region, such as the locally farmed rainbow trout and the pan-seared Springer Mountain airline chicken breast. It's all part of a globally influenced menu chef/owner Danny Mellman seeks to fill with locally sourced ingredients. In fact, Mellman and his partners created a farm to grow their own produce and added chickens and bees for egg and honey production. The interior of the restaurant evokes the feeling of a warm hunting lodge, making it the perfect place for lunch or dinner.

576 E. Main St., Blue Ridge, 706-946-6164
harvestonmain.com

EAT ALFRESCO
AT CAFÉ INTERNATIONAL

There's something about eating a meal outside that makes everything better: The food tastes fresher, the atmosphere seems more relaxed, and the day seems brighter. And at Café International in Helen, not only can you enjoy a menu full of international flavors, but you also can listen to the sounds of the Chattahoochee River as it heads downstream, the waters tumbling over the rocks. For lunch, you can try the Reuben (a house specialty), the French Dip roast beef sandwich, or a German bratwurst with sauerkraut and melted Swiss. Dinner entrées include a German wiener schnitzel, chicken parmigiana, and lemon pepper trout. If visiting the restaurant during the summer, you'll love watching folks float by on their colorful tubes. If visiting during the fall, especially Oktoberfest, get there early or prepare for a wait.

8546 S. Main St., Helen, 706-878-3102
cafeinternationalhelen.com

DINE BY THE WATER
AT THE TOCCOA RIVERSIDE RESTAURANT

If you want dinner (or lunch) with a view, head to the Toccoa Riverside Restaurant in Blue Ridge. Locals rave about the steaks, fresh trout, and fried oysters, all of which make a great dinner. But the lunch menu is equally enticing, with Baja fish tacos, a blackened chicken sandwich, and an exotic burger crafted with wagyu, brisket, and sirloin. Whether you go for lunch or dinner, plan to spend a little extra time enjoying the restaurant's outside deck (Fido is welcome, too!), watching paddlers make their way down the Toccoa River. You can even arrive at the restaurant from the water; diners are welcome to park their canoes and kayaks on the riverbanks while they eat. And if you're looking for the ideal date night spot, this is it.

8055 Aska Rd., Blue Ridge, 706-632-7891
toccoariversiderestaurant.com

SATISFY YOUR SWEET TOOTH
AT LOLLIDROPS SWEET SHOPPE

Opened in 2019, Lollidrops Sweet Shoppe in Jasper didn't waste any time making a name for itself as a top ice-cream parlor. In 2021, it shared top honors as a Best of Georgia™ ice-cream parlor from the *Georgia Business Journal*. Billed as a 1920s-themed ice-cream parlor and candy store, this sweet spot is an ice-cream and candy lover's dream come true. Get a scoop of one of 20 flavors, and enjoy it on a cone, in a milkshake, or in a sundae or banana split. The store also carries a variety of nostalgic candies, including Pop Rocks, candy necklaces, Mary Janes, and many, many more. Lollidrops is the place to reminisce about your childhood favorites, share those memories with your kids, and make new memories with family and friends.

17 S. Main St., Jasper, 706-253-0465
lollidropscandy.com

QUENCH YOUR THIRST
AT REECE'S CIDER CO.

New to the North Georgia Mountains, Reece's Cider Co. in Ellijay puts a new twist on an old favorite: apples. Newly opened in fall 2021, this cidery's primary product is hard apple cider. Not only is that apropos for Gilmer County, the Apple Capital of Georgia, but also for co-owner Taner Reece, who co-founded the cidery with his wife, Sarah. He grew up working in his grandfather's orchard, BJ Reece Orchards, across the street from what's now the cidery. Now, Reece is using his family's apples to craft a new offering for locals and visitors. Visitors can try the hard cider one flavor at a time or sample several with a cider flight. To add to the experience, Reece's Cider Co. often has live music and food trucks on-site, so patrons can kick back and relax for a while.

9110 Hwy. 52 E., Ellijay, 706-635-2775
reecescidercompany.com

FEED YOUR INNER ITALIAN
AT ENRICO'S ITALIAN RESTAURANT

For more than 25 years, this family-owned and -operated Italian restaurant has welcomed its neighbors to dine at its table like family. Menu items range from traditional Italian favorites like chicken parmigiana, linguine with clams, and baked ziti to hand-cut steaks, fresh seafood, and authentic specialty pizzas, all served in a simple, understated dining room. Tucked away at the end of an office complex, this restaurant doesn't overdo it with the bells and whistles, instead letting the food and hospitality speak for themselves. That's what makes it great for everything from a family dinner out to an evening spent with friends to a date night for the two of you. In fact, when planning to visit, always make a reservation for dinner. Otherwise, you may get turned away at the door.

687 Main St., Ste. 5, Young Harris, 706-379-1950
enricositalianrestaurant.com

MAKE TIME FOR LUNCH
AT THE PICNIC CAFÉ & DESSERTERY

A Dahlonega staple since 2001, the Picnic Café & Dessertery offers a menu that would be perfect for, well, a picnic. Selections include a Southern cheddar pimento cheese sandwich, sweet Georgia peach chicken salad, spicy white bean chicken chili, wild rice and mushroom soup, and Brunswick stew. Round out your meal with a sugar cookie or caramel pound cake plus a cup of coffee. The restaurant also has a smaller breakfast menu with such items as breakfast sandwiches, fresh fruit plate, and muffins. Eating your meal at the restaurant is an enjoyable experience, but don't be afraid to get it to go so you can head out for a picnic. Yes, I said it. But am I wrong? If so, I don't want to be right.

30 Public Square N., Dahlonega, 706-864-1095
thepicniccafe.wixsite.com/picniccafe

TAKE IN THE VIEW
AT THE ROOF

A rarity in the North Georgia Mountains, the Roof lives up to its name, offering a dining experience above the streets of downtown Ellijay. This restaurant shares rare air with just a handful of other rooftop eateries in the North Georgia Mountains. Just as unique is the seasonal menu, which features such culinary treats as bologna sliders, the blue oyster mushroom ragu meatloaf, and the Alabama white BBQ slaw. Diners can enjoy their meal inside on cool or rainy days, but the prime location is the restaurant's outdoor dining room. It's the perfect spot to enjoy a cocktail, whether on a clear, sunny day or under the lights once the sun has set. Finding the restaurant entrance can be tricky for some, but just take a stroll around the building to the back, where you'll find a staircase and elevator that will deliver you to the Roof.

16 River St., Ellijay, 706-635-7663
theroofellijay.com

TIP

Parking by the restaurant is minimal, but there is a public parking lot across the street. If that one is full, you may need to drive across the square to a second public parking lot. It's less than a five-minute walk to the restaurant, and gives you a good opportunity to do some window shopping.

OTHER NORTH GEORGIA ROOFTOP EATERIES

Sky Bar, Valhalla Resort Hotel
688 Bahn Innsbruck, Helen
706-878-2200
valhallaresorthotel.com/north-georgia-restaurants/sky-bar

Hook & Eye at Hampton Inn Blue Ridge
50 W. Main St., Blue Ridge
706-642-9001
hookandeyeblueridge.com

GRAB A BURGER
AT UNIVERSAL JOINT

Universal Joint in Clayton epitomizes your local neighborhood hangout. Housed in an old gas station with a large inside dining room, Universal Joint's main attraction—other than the food—is the dog-friendly patio out front. This is the place to be when the weather allows, relaxing with your friends. Menu items include handcrafted burgers, sandwiches, quesadillas, tacos, salads, and a healthy selection of appetizers. All this can be paired with the bar menu of rotating draft beers and specialty cocktails. It's the perfect mix to enjoy while watching your favorite team play on one of the TVs or soaking up the sunshine with the kids. The patio also provides an ideal perch for people-watching, both around the patio and along the street as passersby stroll past. What could be more fun than that?

109 N. Main St., Clayton, 706-782-7116
ujclayton.com

SAMPLE THE HARVEST OF THE SEA
AT MIKE'S SEAFOOD MARKET & GRILL

The North Georgia Mountains might not be near the coastline, but that doesn't mean you can't enjoy the harvest of the sea. At Mike's Seafood Market & Grill in Blairsville, you can fill your plate with crab, lobster, mahi-mahi, swordfish, scallops, grouper, shrimp, snapper, and much more. All come with hush puppies, and you can choose your preferred side dish from such options as garlic cheese grits, cole slaw, onion rings, baked beans, and French fries. If there's a landlubber in your party, they can choose from such items as steak, chicken, or a burger. If you prefer to cook your catch at home, you can pick up something from the seafood market. Choices range from fresh fish, shrimp, and scallops to oysters, clams, crawfish, frog legs, and alligator. You may not be near the coast, but you can still enjoy your favorite seafood!

40A Butternut Crossing, Blairsville, 706-745-9519
mikesseafoodblairsville.com

TASTE A BIT OF NEW ORLEANS
AT THE BOURBON STREET GRILLE

If you're a fan of Cajun cuisine but don't have the time to travel to the Big Easy for an authentic meal, the Bourbon Street Grille in Dahlonega offers what you want. From gator bites to shrimp and crawfish étouffée, jambalaya to red beans and rice, and so much more, there are a lot of Louisiana-inspired dishes here to keep your taste buds jumping. You can even eat on the upstairs balcony overlooking the square in downtown Dahlonega, watching the activity below. While it may not be quite the same as eating on a balcony overlooking Bourbon Street—and the activity may not be quite as colorful as that in the French Quarter—it can be just as enjoyable. Plus, you can wrap up your meal with beignets or bananas Foster. What could be better than that?

90 Public Square N., Dahlonega, 706-864-0086
thebourbonstreetgrille.com

INDULGE IN A CUPCAKE
AT THE SWEET SHOPPE OF THE SOUTH

Who doesn't love a decadent cupcake? These delicious little treats are perfect for satisfying your sweet tooth. And the Sweet Shoppe of the South is just the spot to provide what you want. Think red velvet, turtle, peanut butter cup, cookies and cream, and many, many more. Of course, there's also the S'mores cupcake, which garnered the win on season six of Food Network's *Cupcake Wars* for owners Nikki Kaylor and Susan Catron. And while cupcakes may be the Sweet Shoppe of the South's major claim to fame, it's certainly not the only one. This bakery also specializes in old-fashioned cakes like strawberry, German chocolate, and carrot cake. Or you could choose a cheesecake. Or chocolate-dipped strawberries. Or made-from-scratch cookies. Or pumpkin or pecan pie. In fact, there's so much to choose from, you may have to return again and again to try it all.

721 E. Main St., Blue Ridge, 706-632-6886
thesweetsouth.com

GRAB YOUR FAVORITE CUP OF JOE
AT THE ELLIJAY COFFEEHOUSE

There's nothing better than a local hangout where you can relax with your favorite coffee, latte, cup of tea, or smoothie. And the Ellijay Coffeehouse is just that. Whether meeting friends for lunch—there's a great menu of sandwiches and salads—or enjoying a few moments of alone time, Ellijay Coffeehouse invites you to grab a seat at one of the tables, on the couch in the "living room," or out back on the patio. There's no rush here to get in, eat or drink, and get out. Instead, visitors are invited to "eat, drink, and gather." It's a welcome change from the hustle and bustle of other dining establishments. So stop by, bring a good book or a good friend, order some lunch or a drink, and stay a while.

131 N. Main St., Ellijay, 706-635-5565
ellijaycoffeehouse.com

FEEL LIKE FAMILY
AT BLEU CANOE RESTAURANT & CAMPGROUND

Considered one of the best-kept secrets in the North Georgia Mountains, Bleu Canoe Restaurant & Campground in Clarkesville is tucked away near the south end of Lake Burton. Tiny historic fish-camp cabins and RVs surround the restaurant. Open year-round, it features an outside bar and huge, heated deck. Diners are greeted by not only the owners but also their pets as if you are attending a family reunion. Influenced by Cajun and Creole cuisine, the menu is full of Louisiana favorites, including oysters Rockefeller, shrimp Creole, andouille po-boy, and much more. Something not to miss? The Cajun popcorn, seasoned and lightly fried crawfish tails served with roasted red pepper caper tartar sauce. If the food beckons you to extend your visit, you can book a stay at one of the eclectic accommodations at the adjoining campground. Who wouldn't want to stay in a cute cabin or tiny home?

115 Sweetwater Cir., Clarkesville, 706-947-1833
bleucanoe.com

FEED YOUR LOVE OF CHOCOLATE
AT THE FUDGE FACTORY

Since 1982, the Fudge Factory has delivered sweet treats from the corner of the Dahlonega square that have gone above and beyond satisfying any sweet tooth. As the name implies, fudge is the star of this decadent show, with more than 12 flavors including chocolate, dark chocolate, milk chocolate, chocolate strawberry, butter brickle, maple walnut, and Rocky Road, among others. Alongside the fudge, you'll find such delights as white chocolate pecan nuggets, pecan brittle, truffles, caramel apples, and more. Of course, you couldn't possibly try all of these during just one visit unless you want to end up in a sugar coma. Therefore, you have a ready-made excuse to return again and again so you can sample all you want without destroying your healthy eating habits. Pacing yourself is definitely the way to go.

8 N. Park St., Dahlonega, 706-864-3988
dahlonegafudgefactory.com

ENJOY MORE THAN JUST SANDWICHES
AT SCHROEDER'S NEW DELI

When Schroeder's New Deli first opened in 1981, the menu focused on sandwiches (obviously), nachos, and salads. In the ensuing years, though, that menu would expand to include pizza, calzones, and wings, plus tasty appetizers such as potato skins and fried mushrooms. Sandwich choices include the French Dip, the Italian, a grilled chicken pita, a Turkish sub, and a Pita Max. It's a satisfying menu to say the least. And it's the perfect accompaniment to the restaurant itself. Relaxed, laid-back, and filled with music pumping from the jukebox, Schroeder's New Deli could be described as a hangout for the college kids from nearby Berry College and Shorter University. But locals and visitors of all ages return to this eclectic eatery again and again, so it must be the good food and great atmosphere, right?

406 Broad St., Rome, 706-234-4613
schroedersnewdeli.com

Photo credit: Len Garrison, Seeing Southern

MUSIC
AND ENTERTAINMENT

CATCH LIVE TUNES
AT TOONEYS

While there are opportunities to see live music at venues throughout the North Georgia Mountains, Tooneys Music Venue in McCaysville is one of the few places you can find consistent live music week in and week out. Performers take the stage every Friday and Saturday night, bringing you some of the best musical styles by both local and traveling artists. Think you've got what it takes to join them? Tooneys hosts an open-mic night every Thursday night, where each performer gets their 15 minutes of fame. In addition, Tooneys hosts special events throughout the year to keep the music playing. The venue also features a bar where you can get your favorite beer or wine to enjoy with the music. While Tooneys doesn't offer food, you can grab a meal before a show at one of the restaurants in the neighboring Riverwalk Shops.

100 Blue Ridge Dr., McCaysville, 706-400-6679
tooneys.com

HEAD TO A CONCERT
AT THE GEORGIA
MOUNTAIN FAIRGROUNDS

Touted as the "Country Music Capital of Georgia," the Georgia Mountain Fairgrounds in Hiawassee hosts a full slate of live music events throughout the year. Stars past and present take the stage to bring you not only country music, but also bluegrass, Southern rock, Americana, gospel, and more. Artists who have graced the stage include the Oak Ridge Boys, Vince Gill, Bill Gaither and the Gaither Vocal Band, The Temptations, Three Dog Night, Ronnie Milsap, Josh Turner, and Lee Greenwood. Many of these concerts are standalone events, while others are part of festivals, seasonal events, and, of course, the annual Georgia Mountain Fair. They are a great way to come together with friends, kick up your heels, and lose yourself in the music you love.

1311 Music Hall Rd., Hiawassee, 706-896-4191
georgiamountainfairgrounds.com

HEAR THE RHYTHM
AT CANOPY + THE ROOTS

When it comes to live entertainment, Canopy + the Roots in Dahlonega offers a full schedule of live music, comedy, and the spoken word. Folks are invited to grab a seat in the underground speakeasy listening room to hear from local, regional, and national talent. Come early to enjoy a cup of Costa Rican coffee upstairs in the social house, or grab a beer or glass of wine downstairs while watching the performers. Check the calendar on the website for upcoming shows and get your tickets. When the stage is silent, you can participate in one of Canopy + the Roots' yoga sessions that include Christ-centered, restorative, slow-stretch, and basic vinyasa yoga. It's a great way to clear your mind and body before taking in a night of entertainment.

53 W. Main St., Dahlonega, 706-864-7075
canopyandtheroots.com

COMPETE TO WIN
THE GEORGIA'S ROME SCAVENGER HUNT

Looking for activity that is fun, educational, and gets you outside? Look no further than Georgia's Rome Scavenger Hunt. With three different scavenger hunts to choose from, each challenge takes approximately 35 to 40 minutes, and covers either downtown Rome or the river walk. Each one has a starting point and directs you to the next point of interest, asking a question you must answer to qualify as finding the item. Once you complete the scavenger hunt, you can return your form to the Rome Welcome Center to claim a prize. Forms are available at the welcome center or online. So take the kids or grab your friends and get ready to see who can complete the scavenger hunt first. Winner gets bragging rights!

402 Civic Center Dr., Rome, 706-295-5576
romegeorgia.org/attraction/georgias-rome-scavenger-hunt

WATCH THE LATEST BLOCKBUSTER
AT THE SWAN DRIVE-IN THEATRE

A mainstay of Blue Ridge since 1955, the historic Swan Drive-In Theatre continues to welcome visitors from near and far to watch the new releases on its big screen from the comfort of their cars. This nostalgic moviegoing experience is rare, with just four other drive-in theaters available in Georgia. Depending on the scheduling, you can take in one movie or stick around for a double feature. Going to the drive-in truly is a wonderful way to spend family night with the kids, enjoy a date night, or hang out with your friends. After all, it takes "we're going to the movies" to an entirely new level. It's also one of the best ways to create new memories everyone is sure to remember for a long time.

651 Summit St., Blue Ridge, 706-632-5235
swan-drive-in.com

TIP

You also can catch a movie at these
North Georgia drive-ins:

Tiger Drive-In Theater
2956 Old 441 S., Tiger
706-782-1611, tigerdrivein.com

Wilderness Outdoor Movie Theater
217 Old Hales Gap Rd., Trenton
706-657-8411, wildernesstheater.com

TAKE IN A PLAY
AT A COMMUNITY THEATER

If you've never been to a local theater production, you have been missing out on some quality entertainment. Community theaters are full of talented actors, musicians, dancers, writers, set designers, and so many more behind-the-scenes players, and the Gilmer Arts Community Theatre is no different. Every year, this group puts on a season of performance arts at the Georgia Link Jr. Gilmer Arts Playhouse that will have you laughing, crying, and enjoying an evening of entertaining action. Likewise, the Blue Ridge Community Theater also maintains a full schedule of performances to keep you entertained. Here, performers light up the Main Stage as well as the more intimate Black Box Theater. Comedies, dramas, musicals, and more—it's a whole world of make-believe that will keep you coming back for more.

Gilmer Arts Community Theatre
135 Dalton St., Ellijay, 706-635-5626
gilmerarts.com

Blue Ridge Community Theater
2591 E. First St., Blue Ridge, 706-632-9191
blueridgecommunitytheater.com

GET SPOOKED
ON THE HISTORIC GHOST TOUR

Who doesn't love a good old-fashioned ghost story? With Dahlonega Walking Tours, you can embark on the Historic Ghost Tour and see if you can scare up some otherworldly spirits. Covering 1.5 miles, this tour contains approximately 15 stops, including the historic courthouse, the Crimson Moon (the town's most haunted restaurant), the Vickery House, and the University of North Georgia. The tour highlights Dahlonega's history as the tribal home of the Eastern Cherokee Nation, the site of America's first gold rush, and its role in the Civil War. It all makes for a haunted evening you won't forget. And if you want more, you can check out some of the other tours, such as the Boos and Brews Pub Crawl, Grapes and Ghosts Wine Tour, and Paranormal Investigation Tour.

19 E. Main St., Upstairs Porch, Ste. F, Dahlonega, 706-482-8795
dahlonegawalkingtours.com

CELEBRATE
ALL THINGS APPLE AT THE GEORGIA APPLE FESTIVAL

A North Georgia Mountains mainstay for more than 50 years, the Georgia Apple Festival welcomes 50,000 visitors during the second and third weekends of October to get their fill of all things apple. More than 300 vendors descend upon the Ellijay Lions Club Fairgrounds with a variety of food, arts, crafts, and more. While there will be plenty of apple pastries, apple slushies, and lots and lots of apples, it's also a great place to indulge in everything from mini-doughnuts to barbecue to fried Oreos, and much, much more. When you're not eating, you can check out the many handcrafted items, including pottery, jewelry, woodworking, yard art, and more. In addition to the festival itself, you also don't want to miss the Apple Festival Parade, Apple Festival 5K Road Race, Apple Classic Auto Show, and Apple Arts, an arts and crafts show.

1729 S. Main St., Ellijay, 706-636-4500
georgiaapplefestival.org

TIP

While there is parking at the fairgrounds, it is very limited. Instead, park at one of the off-site lots and take the free shuttles, which will drop you off right at the front gate of the festival. Check the website for current shuttle parking areas.

PRACTICE YOUR SKILL
AT THROWING AXES

Gaining popularity throughout the North Georgia Mountains, axe throwing is the new way to spend time with friends or on a date. While it might sound crazy, especially since most venues also serve alcohol, axe throwing is actually a fun, safe way to spend time together. Similar to darts, this activity involves participants who throw an axe from a specified distance and try to hit the target on the bull's-eye. Obviously, for many, this is going to take some practice, which means there will be a lot of laughs as you try to figure it out. Once you get the hang of it, the real fun begins: competing with one another to see who wins the game. And in the North Georgia Mountains, you don't have to go far to find a place to throw your own axe.

Axe Throwing Therapy
322 W. Main St., Blue Ridge, 706-403-2418
axethrowingtherapy.com

AxeBilly
8160 S. Main St., Helen, 706-878-0003
axebilly.com

Ellijay Axes
941 Maddox Dr., Suite 216, Ellijay, 706-502-7070
ellijayaxes.com

The Axe Armory
121 Hodges St., Cornelia, 762-230-1336
theaxearmory.com

DON YOUR LEDERHOSEN
FOR HELEN'S OKTOBERFEST

Everybody loves a good celebration, and Oktoberfest in Helen is not just a good time, it's a great time. Originating in Germany, this two-month celebration of beer, brats, and lederhosen brings together German-style bands and dancing with delicious food into a fun-filled festival. You can get the party started at the Oktoberfest parade before kicking up your heels at the Helen Festhalle. Even the kids can take part in this event with their own dance floor. While activities take place throughout the entire two months, you can visit for a day, a weekend, or longer. Just keep in mind this is Helen's busiest time of the year, so plan accordingly to make sure you have the time you want to enjoy the festival. If you plan to stay overnight, make your reservations early as accommodations book up fast.

1074 Edelweiss Strasse, Helen, 706-878-1619
helenchamber.com/oktoberfest-menu/oktoberfest-info.html

PICK A PUMPKIN
AT BURT'S PUMPKIN FARM

The North Georgia Mountains remain a popular destination for all things fall, and that includes picking a pumpkin—or two, three, or more—at Burt's Pumpkin Farm in Dawsonville. You'll find pumpkins of all sizes, ranging from a few ounces to a few hundred pounds, that are perfect for fall decorating, making jack-o'-lanterns, and even baking pies. But wait! There's more! Head to the largest pumpkins in the patch for some great photo ops (just don't sit or climb on the pumpkins, please), or stop by the tractor for a quick snap. In fact, you'll find several photo-op spots around the farm, so see how many you can find. Just make sure you save time for a hayride around the farm. And, before you head out with your pumpkins, swing through the farm store for fresh produce, baked goods, and other delicious treats.

5 Burt's Farm Rd., Dawsonville, 800-600-2878
burtsfarm.com

SIT IN
ON AN OLD-FASHIONED
APPALACHIAN JAM SESSION

Gathering with friends, family, and neighbors for an afternoon of playing music and singing has been a favorite pastime in the communities of the North Georgia Mountains for decades. That tradition continues with Appalachian Jam every Saturday afternoon in April through October from 2 to 4 p.m. at the Dahlonega Gold Museum State Historic Site in downtown Dahlonega. Everyone is invited to bring their own instruments, chime in on a song, do a little dance, and enjoy the merriment of these impromptu concerts. Not only do these events help preserve this pastime for generations to come, but they also go a long way in turning strangers into friends. It might seem daunting to pull up a chair, start picking or singing, and become a part of the action, but it'll be an experience you won't forget. And, more than likely, you'll be back for more on the next Saturday.

1 Public Square, Dahlonega
facebook.com/DahlonegaAppalachianJam

FIND YOUR WAY
THROUGH UNCLE SHUCK'S CORN MAZE

Who doesn't love getting lost in a good corn maze on a beautiful fall day? For those who do, Uncle Shuck's features a 15-acre corn maze with approximately 6 miles of trails. But working your way through the corn maze is not just about finding your way from the entrance to the exit. Along the way, there are checkpoints to mark off as you go through, so the fun is trying to find them all without getting lost. Take it to the next level by breaking into teams to see who can find them first. Just make sure you have a teammate who can read the maze map. (Easier said than done!) Once you find your way out, there's more fun to be had. Jump on the wagon ride, shoot some corn from the corn cannon, watch kids climb the tire mountain, and snap photos at the many photo props.

125 Bannister Rd., Dawsonville, 770-772-6223
uncleshucks.com

STROLL THE STREETS OF DAHLONEGA
DURING GOLD RUSH DAYS

Every third full weekend of October, more than 200,000 locals and visitors head to Dahlonega for a mix of arts and crafts, fair foods, live music, and more during Gold Rush Days. More than 200 vendors set up on the streets around the square and throughout the Historic District, where you can stroll by and check out their wares. Both days feature a full schedule of performances by musicians, dance groups, artisans, and others. On Saturday afternoon, you also can catch the coronation of the Gold Rush Days king and queen as well as the parade. Whether you come for the day or stay for the weekend, it's a fun-filled event that could quickly become a family tradition year after year.

1 Public Square, Dahlonega
goldrushdaysfestival.com

TIP

Dahlonega is a great place to visit any time of the year. From Bear on the Square to The Festival of Arts and Wine to the Mountain Top Rodeo there are events throughout the year. Check out dahlonega.org/event for a list of events during your visit.

TIP

Parking is at a premium during Gold Rush Days, so park in the designated lots on the University of North Georgia campus. Streets can and do get very crowded, so pack your patience and take your time as you enjoy the festival.

SPORTS
AND RECREATION

40

CHECK OUT
THE REGION'S WATERFALLS

Throughout the North Georgia Mountains, you'll find scenic waterfalls cascading down through the trees and over the rocks. Many of these waterfalls are located within Georgia State Parks. Some are easily accessible, while others are found at the end of hiking trails, some more strenuous than others. The joy is you get to pick which ones you want to tackle. For instance, Amicalola Falls, the tallest cascading waterfall in the Southeast, is located in Amicalola Falls State Park near Dawsonville. You can hike up the 604 steps from the bottom to the viewing platform, you can access the ADA-accessible West Ridge Trail to the viewing platform, or you can view the falls from the top. At Black Rock Mountain State Park in Mountain City, you can climb a short but steep trail to the Ada-Hi Falls. With so many waterfalls, you can return again and again to see them all.

TIP
To find more waterfalls in Georgia State Parks, visit gastateparks.org and enter "waterfalls" in the search bar at the top right of the page.

Amicalola Falls State Park
418 Amicalola Falls Rd., Dawsonville
800-573-9656
amicalolafallslodge.com

Black Rock Mountain State Park
3085 Black Rock Mountain Pkwy., Mountain City
706-746-2141
gastateparks.org/BlackRockMountain

41

HIKE THE APPALACHIAN TRAIL
IN THE NORTH GEORGIA MOUNTAINS

One of the best ways to take in the beauty of the North Georgia Mountains is by hiking some of the hundreds of miles of trails that traverse the region. And what better trail to start with than the Appalachian Trail? The southern terminus of the Appalachian Trail is located at Springer Mountain in Fannin County. You can reach Springer Mountain from Forest Service Road 42, where you will embark on a 0.9-mile hike south to the summit of Springer Mountain. If you're up for the challenge, you can start in Amicalola Falls State Park, where you'll find an 8.5-mile approach trail that begins behind the visitors center. The Appalachian Trail covers 78.1 miles in Georgia, but you don't have to hike that far if you don't want. Hike a little, or hike a lot; it's your choice. Whatever you decide, you can always say you hiked the Appalachian Trail.

Forest Service Road 42
fs.usda.gov/recarea/conf/recreation/hiking/recarea/?recid=10539&actid=50

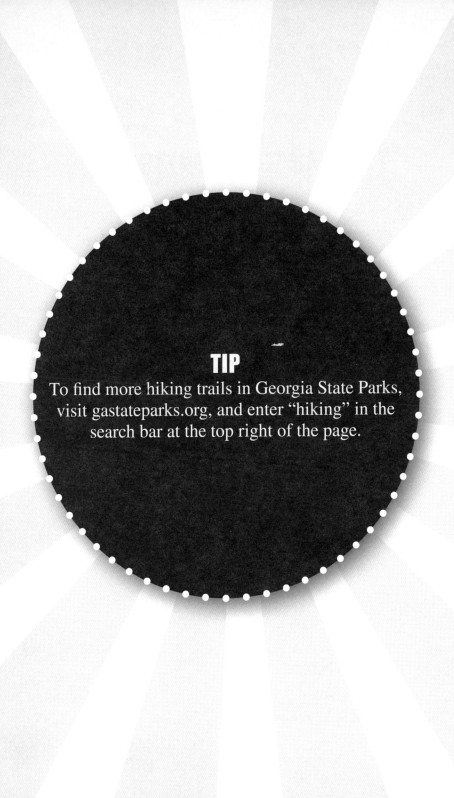

TIP

To find more hiking trails in Georgia State Parks, visit gastateparks.org, and enter "hiking" in the search bar at the top right of the page.

ZIP
THROUGH THE MOUNTAIN AIR

There's nothing better than strapping into a harness, snapping into a zip trolley, and flying through the air along a zip line. Actually, that's not true. There's nothing better than zip lining across the North Georgia Mountains over treetops, rivers, creeks, and mountainsides. You don't have to be an adrenaline junkie to feel the rush of excitement as you reach speeds up to 30 to 40 mph. But many zip-line tours are more than just flying through the air. Many also include sky bridges, suspension bridges, rappelling decks, and other obstacles that provide not only fun challenges but also additional unique views of the mountains. Take the kids, take some friends—but make sure you bring your sense of adventure. If you do, you won't be disappointed!

Amicalola Falls State Park
418 Amicalola Falls Rd., Dawsonville
800-573-9656
amicalolafallslodge.com/adventures/zip-lines

Nacoochee Adventures
7019 S. Main St., Helen
706-878-9477
nacoocheeadventures.com

Sunburst Adventures
251 Sunburst Lane, Clarkesville
706-947-7433
sunburststables.com

Unicoi State Park
1788 Highway 356, Helen
800-573-9659
unicoilodge.com/adventures/zip-lines

Zipline Canopy Tours of Blue Ridge
891 Old Cashes Valley Rd., Blue Ridge
800-251-4800
zipblueridge.com

43

CRUSH SOME CARS
AT TANK TOWN USA

Have you ever dreamed of conquering the landscape in a military tank? Digging in the dirt with a construction excavator? You can do just that at Tank Town USA in Morganton. Once you complete the personal instruction, you're ready to take the wheel and drive the tank over bumps, dips, and humps. If you go after it rains, so much the better because the mud adds a fun factor that elevates your experience to the next level. For the ultimate thrill, though, you can upgrade your experience to do more than just traverse the landscape. You can crush a car! Who doesn't want to feel the power of crushing steel and shattering glass? Of course, if you prefer something a little less destructive, you can try your hand at running the construction excavator, digging and moving dirt around. For the best of both, sign up for a combo package!

10408 Appalachian Hwy., Morganton, 706-633-6072
tanktownusa.com

Photo credit: Len Garrison, Seeing Southern

44

TACKLE
THE MOUNTAIN BIKING CAPITAL OF GEORGIA THANKS TO MULBERRY GAP

With more than 100 miles of singletrack, Gilmer County is much more than the Apple Capital of Georgia. It's also the Mountain Biking Capital of Georgia. From easy cross-country trails to technical downhills, there are trails for every skill level from beginners to experts. It's a fun yet challenging way to explore the mountains with new adventures around every corner. A great place to start is Mulberry Gap, a one-stop shop for mountain biking. If you're just getting started, you can begin with a day pass that includes access to such facilities as secure parking, bathrooms, bike wash, trail maps, and more. Feel like extending your adventure? You can book a cabin or campsite for a weekend or longer. One thing to keep in mind when mountain biking: You're sharing the woods with wildlife, so maintain a watchful eye and keep your distance if you encounter the locals.

400 Mulberry Gap Rd., Ellijay, 706-698-2865
mulberrygap.com

TIP

If your gear needs attention, you want some new accessories, or you're in the market for new bikes, check out Cartecay Bike Shop in Ellijay.

493 N. Main St.
706-635-2453
cartecaybikes.com

45

RACE YOUR FRIENDS
AT ATLANTA MOTORSPORTS PARK

Do you have a need for speed that has gone unfulfilled for far too long? Then hitting the track at Atlanta Motorsports Park in Dawsonville has just what you need. This is not your ordinary go-kart track at the local mini-golf attraction or even like the multi-level go-kart tracks found at many beach destinations. The track at AMP was designed and built to Formula One standards, meaning it has numerous challenging turns and 43 feet of elevation change. And with karts reaching speeds up to 55 mph, your adrenaline better be in full supply! Drivers must be at least 12 years old (and 50 inches tall), so this can be the next big family adventure on your calendar. To make sure you hit the track, though, it's important to make reservations so you don't get stuck waiting for your turn behind the wheel.

20 Duck Thurmond Rd., Dawsonville, 678-381-8526
atlantamotorsportspark.com

FIND SERENITY IN NATURE
AT GIBBS GARDENS

If you love all things garden, you can't miss Gibbs Gardens in Ball Ground. Covering 336 acres with five featured gardens and 21 seasonal collections gardens, there's so much to see and experience. In fact, the recommended time for a visit is four hours. And you'll want every minute to take in the natural beauty. While walking through the gardens provides scenic views at every turn, some of the best moments come when you take a seat on one of the many benches and absorb the sights and smells around you. The warm sunshine, the light breeze, the hum of conversation from other garden visitors; it all coalesces into a peace that could only come from nature. From daffodils in the spring to hydrangeas in the summer to Japanese maples in the fall, there's always something gorgeous waiting for you.

1987 Gibbs Dr., Ball Ground, 770-893-1880
gibbsgardens.com

FEEL THE RUSH
OF THE GEORGIA MOUNTAIN COASTER

If you haven't taken a ride on an alpine coaster, have you really lived at all? What makes it different than a regular roller coaster? An alpine coaster uses the land's natural elevation along with gravity to carry riders from the top of the track to the bottom. Riders sit in a cart similar to a bobsled instead of a train of attached cars, and they can control their speed using a manual brake. It takes a minute or two to get the hang of it, but once you do, you are ready to let loose and enjoy the ride. Obviously, while it's not going to provide the same type of thrills as a theme-park roller coaster, riding an alpine roller coaster such as the Georgia Mountain Coaster in Helen is one of the most fun experiences you'll ever have.

8409 S. Main St., Helen, 706-878-1347
georgiamountaincoaster.com

CONQUER THE RAPIDS
WITH WHITEWATER RAFTING

Adventure-seekers will find more than enough adrenaline-pumping action as they embark on whitewater rafting on the Ocoee River. While the trip begins just over the state line in Tennessee, you'll soon travel into Georgia on the same waters that served as the venue for the 1996 Olympics. Every dip, crest, and splash of the waters elicits gasps, squeals, and screams as you work to conquer the Class III and IV rapids. Don't worry, though. Every trip includes the steady hand of an expert guide to help you along the way. You can start by rafting the Middle section, which includes one stretch where you can actually jump out of the raft for a swim, or choose the Upper section, which includes the actual one-mile Olympic course. If you're up for the challenge, you can raft both sections during a full-day trip that includes lunch alongside the river.

Rolling Thunder River Company
20 Hughes St., McCaysville, 800-408-7238
rollingthunderriverco.com

LAND THE BIG ONE
IN THE REGION'S LAKES AND RIVERS

If you haven't enjoyed the serenity of casting a line into water
and waiting for that first wiggle as a fish starts to nibble at the
bait, you don't know what you're missing. Fishing itself provides
hours of quiet time to reflect and become one with nature. It also
presents an opportunity to land the big one and secure bragging
rights with your friends. In the North Georgia Mountains, there's
no shortage of spots to find your trophy fish. The rivers are full
of trout, and the lakes contain plenty of striper, crappie, walleye,
and much more. If you aren't sure where or how to get started,
reach out to one of the expert fishing guides in the North Georgia
Mountains, such as Lake & Stream Guide Service in Ellijay. It
won't be long until you catch that big one—at least, that's how
the story will go, right?

Lake & Stream Guide Service, 706-669-4973
ellijayfishing.com

TIP

Per Georgia state law, everyone age 16 and older must have a current Georgia fishing license to fish in fresh or salt water in the state. To find out more and to purchase a license online, visit georgiawildlife.com/licenses-permits-passes/choose.

SADDLE UP
FOR SOME HORSEBACK RIDING

The North Georgia Mountains offers so many wonderful opportunities to immerse yourself in the great outdoors, and horseback riding is another way to do just that. From taking a guided trail ride with Blue Ridge Mountain Trail Rides to a sunset ride with Sunburst Adventures to a river ride with Dillard House Stables, there's a lot to choose from for your next equestrian adventure. And, as with all outdoor adventures in the North Georgia Mountains, you never know which native residents you'll spot along the way, so keep a close eye out for wildlife. Horseback riding is a wonderful outing for families, but there are some age restrictions so check those out before booking your ride. Remember, too, to dress accordingly so you don't walk away from your ride with unwanted blisters. Your trail guide can tell you the right gear for your outing.

Blue Ridge Mountain Trail Rides
319 Hell's Hollow Rd., Blue Ridge
706-408-7433
blueridgemountaintrailrides.com

Sunburst Adventures
251 Sunburst Ln., Clarkesville
706-947-7433
sunburststables.com

Dillard House Stables
768 Franklin St., Dillard
706-746-2038
dillardhousestables.com

Trackrock Stables
202 Trackrock Camp Rd., Blairsville
706-745-5252
trackrock.com

PRACTICE YOUR AIM
AT ETOWAH VALLEY SPORTING CLAYS

Whether you are just starting out or you've been shooting for years, Etowah Valley Sporting Clays welcomes sport shooters of all skill levels to try your skills on one of its many courses in Dawsonville. With clay, skeet, trap, and five-stand shooting, you'll find a challenge that suits your style and skill level, ensuring you have a good time no matter which you choose. If you've never been before, it can feel a bit uncomfortable and intimidating at the beginning, but following some guidance from the instructors, you'll be hitting targets before you know it. If you want extra one-on-one instruction, you can schedule some private lessons to improve your skills. Bring your family and friends, and see who walks away with bragging rights. At least, until the next time you hit the course.

619 Sporting Hill Dr., Dawsonville, 706-265-1611
etowahvalleysportingclays.com

SHOOT THE HOOCH
WITH COOL RIVER TUBING

One of the best ways to celebrate summer is to shoot the Hooch—the Chattahoochee River, that is—in Helen. At Cool River Tubing, you can choose between a short tubing trip (1 to 1.5 hours) or a long one (2 to 2.5 hours), with both trips taking you through the heart of downtown Helen. Regardless of which one you choose, this is a lot of fun for the whole family. One thing to keep in mind: The water level fluctuates, so the best time to go is after it rains when water levels are higher and you can enjoy more of a float. If you go when the water levels are down, expect to work a little more to keep your tube on the go.

590 Edelweiss Strasse, Helen, 706-878-2665
coolrivertubing.com

HIT THE LAKES
OF THE NORTH GEORGIA MOUNTAINS

The North Georgia Mountains are full of lakes that are ideal for boating enthusiasts. These include Carters Lake, Lake Blue Ridge, Lake Burton, Lake Chatuge, Lake Rabun, Lake Yonah, and Nottely Lake. At the lower fringes of the North Georgia Mountains you'll also find Lake Allatoona and Lake Lanier. All of these lakes welcome boaters who like to water-ski, fish, or just take a scenic ride on the water. In addition, you'll find many quiet spots to throw anchor and go for a swim. Bring along a picnic to make it a full-day adventure. If you don't have your own boat, there are numerous marinas that offer rentals you can take out for a few hours or the entire day.

Carters Lake
sam.usace.army.mil/Missions/Civil-Works/
Recreation/Carters-Lake/

Carters Lake Marina & Resort
575 Marina Rd., Chatsworth, 706-276-4891
carterslake.com

Lake Blue Ridge
blueridgemountains.com/things-to-do/outdoors/water-sports/
lake-blue-ridge

Lake Blue Ridge Marina
335 Marina Dr., Blue Ridge, 706-632-2618
lakeblueridgemarina.com

Lake Burton
georgiapowerlakes.com/northgeorgialakes

LaPrade's Marina
25 Shoreline Tr., Clarkesville, 706-947-0010
lapradesmarina.com

Anchorage Boat Dock
75 Timpson Cove Rd., Clayton, 706-782-3013
anchorageboatdock.com

Lake Chatuge
tourism.golakechatuge.com/list/category/boating-water-sports-
sales-and-service-1185

Lake Rabun
explorerabun.com/lake-rabun

Lake Yonah
georgiapowerlakes.com/northgeorgialakes

Nottely Lake
US Hwy. 19 & 129 N., Blairsville, 706-745-5789
exploregeorgia.org/blairsville/outdoors-nature/fishing/
lake-nottely

Lake Allatoona
allatoonalake.org

Lake Lanier
discoverlakelanier.com/home/play/on-the-lake

SEE SEVEN STATES
AT ONCE FROM ROCK CITY

In the far reaches of the North Georgia Mountains, you'll find Lookout Mountain, home to Rock City. Since 1932, visitors have flocked to this mountaintop attraction to walk among the natural rock formations such as Fat Man's Squeeze, Hall of the Mountain King, and Needle's Eye. Many make their way to Lover's Leap, where you can take in panoramic views of seven states at one time. The grounds also include more than 400 native plants scattered among the rocks and the gardens. Also on-site, you can view handcrafted, larger-than-life dioramas of classic childhood fairy tales showcased with retro glowing paints. Some people think they are interesting, while others think they are creepy. Come take a look, and see what you think. Commemorate your visit with a See Rock City birdhouse or trinket that celebrates the infamous barn advertising campaign of the 1930s.

1400 Patten Rd., Lookout Mountain, 706-820-2531
seerockcity.com

CATCH SOME BASEBALL
WITH THE ROME BRAVES

Although most folks don't think of Rome as a North Georgia Mountains destination, it actually rests in the foothills of the Appalachian Mountains. And calling Rome home is the High-A Affiliate of the Atlanta Braves, the Rome Braves. Taking in a game with the Rome Braves is an intimate, family-friendly outing that gives fans an up close and personal view of the action. With just 5,105 seats, attending a Rome Braves game is like watching the game with your closest friends. And while you get a good look at up-and-coming Braves players, you never know when you might see some Atlanta Braves stars taking the field during a rehab stint. You'll also love the lower prices for game tickets and parking, making this quite the affordable outing.

755 Braves Blvd. N.E., Rome, 706-378-5100
milb.com/rome

CAMP UNDER THE STARS
AT GEORGIA STATE PARKS

Already a popular choice for outdoor recreation, camping continues to grow in popularity with folks looking to enjoy nature. At the Georgia State Parks throughout the North Georgia Mountains, you'll find hundreds of campsites to set up your tent or hook up your RV, all with electrical and water hookups, grills or fire rings, and picnic tables. Other features at many of these campgrounds include modern comfort stations with hot showers, flush toilets, and electrical outlets. For RV visitors, all campgrounds have dump stations, and several even offer cable-TV hookups. For diehard campers, many state parks also offer walk-in and backcountry tent sites. At Fort Mountain and Unicoi state parks, you can camp on a covered platform with just your sleeping bag. No matter which campsite you choose, you can bet you'll have a great night under the stars.

Amicalola Falls State Park
418 Amicalola Falls Rd., Dawsonville, 800-573-9656

Black Rock Mountain State Park
3085 Black Rock Mountain Pkwy., Mountain City, 706-746-2141

Cloudland Canyon State Park
122 Cloudland Canyon Park Rd., Rising Fawn
706-657-4050

Don Carter State Park
5000 North Browning Bridge Rd., Gainesville
678-450-7726

Fort Mountain State Park
181 Fort Mountain Park Rd., Chatsworth
706-422-1932

Moccasin Creek State Park
3655 Hwy. 197, Clarkesville, 706-947-3194

Red Top Mountain State Park
50 Lodge Rd. SE, Acworth, 770-975-0055

Tallulah Gorge State Park
338 Jane Hurt Yarn Dr., Tallulah Falls, 706-754-7981

Unicoi State Park
1788 Hwy. 356, Helen, 800-573-9659

Vogel State Park
405 Vogel State Park Rd., Blairsville, 706-745-2628
gastateparks.org

VISIT GEORGIA'S HIGHEST POINT
AT BRASSTOWN BALD

At 4,784 feet above sea level, Brasstown Bald in the Chattahoochee-Oconee National Forests is the highest point in Georgia. Thankfully, you don't have to hike the entire mountain to check out the view. Instead, you can go to the Brasstown Bald Visitor Center, where you can catch a shuttle to the viewing platform. If you feel the need for some exercise, there is a 0.6-mile paved foot trail that is very steep. Once you do reach the top, you can take in a 360-degree view of the Southern Appalachian Mountains. If the weather is clear, you can even see four states. Inside the visitor center, there is an 8,000-square-foot museum with cultural and natural history exhibits. The visitor center closes during winter, but the trail and observation deck are open year-round. Just check weather conditions before driving up because local roads could be closed.

2941 Hwy. 180 Spur, Hiawassee, 706-896-2556
fs.usda.gov/recarea/conf/recreation/recarea/?recid=10542

FIND SOME TREASURE
WHILE GEOCACHING

Started more than 20 years ago, geocaching is treasure hunting at its best. Geocaches are hidden containers placed along hiking trails, at popular attractions, in downtown hotspots, and other locations for geocachers to find using GPS-capable devices. The containers often contain small trinkets such as stickers, mini toys, coins, and travel bugs. Travel bugs are trackable items that are logged on the Geocaching app so others can see where it has been. In the North Georgia Mountains, there are hundreds of geocaches just waiting to be found. The best way to start is to download and use the Geocaching app, which contains the locations of thousands of geocaches. Another great place to start is at Georgia State Parks & Historic Sites, which have official caches at many locations. It's a great way to get outside and have fun while trying a new adventure.

To get the Geocaching app, visit geocaching.com/play.

To learn more about geocaching in Georgia State Parks & Historic Sites, visit gastateparks.org/Geocaching.

GET UP CLOSE AND PERSONAL
WITH THE ANIMALS AT NORTH GEORGIA WILDLIFE SAFARI PARK

Why go to the zoo and just watch the animals when you can go to North Georgia Wildlife Safari Park in Cleveland and interact with the animals? There are a number of options for the animal encounter you want, depending on just how up close and personal you want to get. For example, you can do a drive-thru safari from the comfort of your own car where you can drive among camels, zebras, ostrich, llamas, and more. For closer encounters, you can sign up for specific animal experiences such as walking among the deer in their habitat or posing for a photo with a camel. For the most intimate encounter, you can sign up for a variety of experiences such as feeding alligators, petting a young wolf, holding a baby kangaroo, or hanging out with a sloth. If you are an avid animal lover, this is the activity for you.

2912 Paradise Valley Rd., Cleveland, 706-348-7279
northgeorgiazoo.com

MINE FOR GEMS
AT THE LILLY PAD VILLAGE

If you've ever dreamed of finding an emerald, sapphire, amethyst, or other gemstone, gem mining at the Lilly Pad Village in Blue Ridge is for you. Here you'll receive a bucket filled with dirt and stones, which you can wash and sort through looking for gems. If you come across something that looks interesting but you aren't sure what it is, the expert staff is on hand to go over your find so you can decide if it's worth keeping. Kids especially will love making new discoveries as the water clears out the dirt, leaving behind a wealth of interesting treasures. Once you've mined all your gems, you can take a break at one of the picnic tables, or move on to one of the Lilly Pad Village's other activities. You can go fishing in the catch-and-release pond or challenge the kids to a round of mini golf.

24 Adelaide Dr., Blue Ridge, 706-534-1317
lillypadvillage.com

SEARCH FOR THE HIDDEN HEART
AT FORT MOUNTAIN STATE PARK

At Fort Mountain State Park near the Cohutta Wilderness, the Civilian Conservation Corps built a 38-foot stone fire tower during the Great Depression. One of the stonemasons, Arnold Bailey, was pining for his sweetheart back home. To honor their love, he carved a heart-shaped stone and placed it above a window. His sweetheart, Margaret Reece, apparently appreciated his gesture. The two were married for 59 years until he passed away in 1994. Visitors to the park can hike the trail to the stone fire tower and see if they can find the duo's symbol of love. In doing so, be sure to look out for the ancient rock wall that stands sentry in the park. No one knows the origins of the 855-foot-long wall, but the general consensus is it could have been built by early Native Americans. Take a look and see what you think.

181 Fort Mountain Park Rd., Chatsworth, 706-422-1932
gastateparks.org/FortMountain

MEET CHARMING ANIMALS
AT LASSO THE MOON ALPACA FARM

Who doesn't want to play with alpacas? Their sweet faces and incredibly soft coats just invite you to say hello. At Lasso the Moon Alpaca Farm, you can take a tour to not only learn about these animals, but also how their fiber coats are processed and used to create clothing as well as fiber art. Scheduled by appointment only via the website, these 45-minute tours are immersive, meaning you can interact with the alpacas in their stalls. The second half of the tour focuses on the alpacas' fiber, and includes a stop in the farm's Lardworks Glass & Fiber studio gallery/store. For those interested in learning more about fiber art, the studio offers classes online and in person. All in all, it's an unusual experience you won't find in too many other places—and one you definitely should not miss.

106 Agape Dr., Blairsville, 706-835-1837
farmfeltandglass.com/visit-the-farm-2

CULTURE AND HISTORY

EXPLORE THE IMPACT OF GRASSROOTS ART
AT THE FOLK POTTERY MUSEUM OF NORTHEAST GEORGIA

Considered one of the South's premier grassroots art forms, much of the original folk pottery initially served as essential household items, but, today, these items are recognized as the folk art they are. Exhibits document 200 years of the area's folk pottery history spotlighting the techniques that go into these pieces, the evolution from functional to decorative items that began in the 1920s, and how face jugs were created. Located at the Sautee Nacoochee Cultural Center, the Folk Pottery Museum is joined by the SNC History Museum and the SNC African-American Heritage Site. These two museums provide a glimpse into the people who lived and worked in this community through various maps, photographs, and articles that document the past. These are valuable assets that preserve the stories of the people of the North Georgia Mountains.

283 Hwy. 255 N., Sautee Nacoochee, 706-878-3300
snca.org

TRACK DOWN SASQUATCH
AT EXPEDITION BIGFOOT

If you've ever caught a glimpse of Bigfoot in the woods or thought you came across Sasquatch's footprints, you are not alone. Expedition Bigfoot: The Sasquatch Museum between Ellijay and Blue Ridge shares exhibits that contain evidence and witness testimony from personal experiences and encounters with Bigfoot. For instance, you can see the country's largest collection of footprint casts, hear recordings of possible Bigfoot growls, and check out the world's only Bigfoot research and tech vehicle. Is he real? Is he fake? Visit, check it out, and decide for yourself. And if you have your own personal experience to share, feel free to share it with museum personnel. The museum also is a research and reporting center, so all evidence and testimonies are welcome.

1934 Hwy. 515, Blue Ridge, 706-946-2601
expeditionbigfoot.com

ENJOY THE VIEWS
FROM THE ETOWAH INDIAN MOUNDS

Sitting alongside the Etowah River near Cartersville in the foothills of the Appalachian Mountains, the Etowah Indian Mounds State Historic Site features six earthen mounds on 54 acres. Believed to be the home of Native Americans from 1000 A.D. to 1550 A.D., the Etowah Indian Mounds are the most intact Mississippian culture site in the Southeast. Only a small part has been excavated in an effort to learn about the people who lived here, and that information is shared through exhibits and displays as well as an informative movie in the visitors center. From the visitors center, you can take a nature trail out to the different mounds, where you can climb the staircases to take in the views at the top. The nature trail also takes you down by the Etowah River where you can see a V-shaped fish trap in the water.

813 Indian Mounds Rd. SE, Cartersville, 770-387-3747
gastateparks.org/EtowahIndianMounds

DELVE INTO RACING HISTORY
AT THE GEORGIA RACING HALL OF FAME

Racing fans will love the displays and exhibits that tell the story of racing as it evolved from moonshiners running the roads of the North Georgia Mountains in the 1930s to the NASCAR Cup champions of the modern racing era. Displays range from a 1935 Ford-powered Sprint car used to run shine to the evolution of the racing tire to the Jimmy Mosteller and Captain Herb Library, where you can dig deeper into racing history. A big portion of the facility is devoted to the Elliott family, Dawsonville's racing dynasty that began with Erving George Elliott Jr., and includes 1988 NASCAR Cup champion Bill Elliott (George's son) and 2020 NASCAR Cup champion Chase Elliott (Bill's son). Of course, you also can see the display of each member of the Georgia Racing Hall of Fame. Every year, new members are inducted based on their significant and/or long-term contributions to motorsports in Georgia.

415 Hwy. 53 E., Dawsonville, 706-216-7223
georgiaracinghof.com

ADOPT A CABBAGE PATCH KID
AT BABYLAND GENERAL

Starting in 1976, Xavier Roberts created Little People Originals using a German technique for fabric sculpture known as needle molding. In 1978, Roberts started to sell his dolls for an "adoption fee." The response was impressive; therefore, Roberts opened BabyLand General Hospital so people could come see and adopt their own dolls. When the demand for the Little People Originals expanded beyond Georgia in the early 1980s, they were licensed under the Cabbage Patch Kids name and skyrocketed in the toy market. Today, you can still purchase (adopt) a hand-sculpted doll at BabyLand General Hospital in Cleveland. Visitors can take a tour of the hospital, learning the dolls' history and witnessing a live birth of a doll with Mother Cabbage beneath the branches of the Magic Crystal Tree. While this is a big draw for families, it's a fun stop for anyone who ever had or loved Cabbage Patch Kids.

300 N. O. K. Dr., Cleveland, 706-865-2171
cabbagepatchkids.com/pages/babyland-general-hospital

CELEBRATE THE CHEROKEE PEOPLE
AT NEW ECHOTA

In the foothills of the Appalachian Mountains, New Echota is both a haunting and much-needed educational site. New Echota once was the capital of the thriving Cherokee Nation, but it also is the site where the Trail of Tears officially began. Today, the site contains 12 original and reconstructed buildings from the original city. These include the courthouse, Council House, an 1805 store, a print shop, and missionary Samuel Worchester's home. At the visitor center, you can watch a 17-minute film that shares the history of New Echota, before moving on to see interpretive exhibits on the people who lived here. You can take a self-guided tour or call for a schedule of upcoming guided tours. Before leaving, take some time to explore the nature trails that lead to New Town Creek and a small beaver pond. You might be surprised at what you see.

1211 Chatsworth Hwy. NE, Calhoun, 706-624-1321
gastateparks.org/NewEchota

CLIMB ABOARD
THE BLUE RIDGE SCENIC RAILWAY

Hop on a vintage train for a 26-mile roundtrip journey to McCaysville and back to Blue Ridge. Along the way, you'll take in views of the North Georgia Mountains countryside and the Toccoa River. Be sure to watch for the V-shaped rock formation in the water that served as a fish trap for Native Americans. The actual train excursion is two hours round trip, but you'll have a two-hour layover in the neighboring towns of McCaysville and Copperhill, Tenn. The Georgia-Tennessee state line actually runs through the middle of town, so make sure you snap a photo at the state line marker as you stand in two places at once. The train features both open-air coach cars and climate-controlled closed cars; if the weather is nice, it's highly recommended to sit in the open-air cars for a more immersive experience.

241 Depot St., Blue Ridge, 877-413-8724
brscenic.com

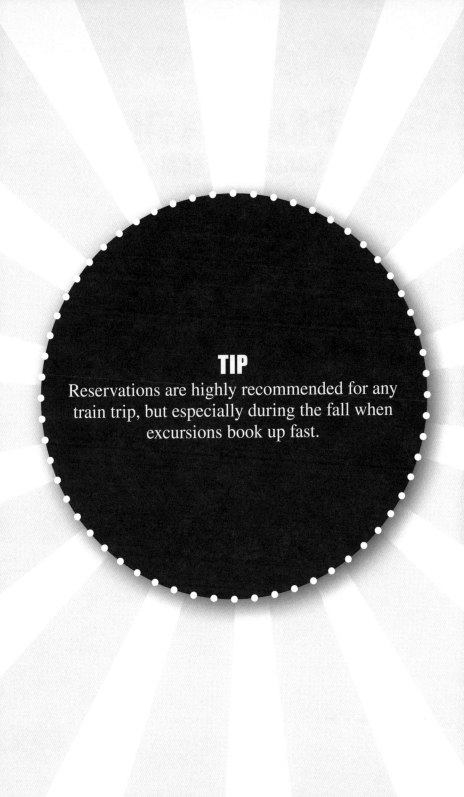

TIP

Reservations are highly recommended for any train trip, but especially during the fall when excursions book up fast.

STEP BACK IN TIME
AT THE HARDMAN FARM STATE HISTORIC SITE

Built in 1870, Hardman Farm includes 23 structures, not the least of which is the farmhouse, a stellar example of Italianate architecture. The home was built by Col. James Nichols (who insisted he be called "Captain"), and the home tour includes a look at his daughter's room. Anna Ruby Nichols is the namesake for nearby Anna Ruby Falls. The second owner, Calvin Hunnicutt, used the home as a summer retreat and left behind many of his original furnishings. It was the farm's third owner, Georgia Gov. Dr. Lamartine Hardman, who donated the property to the state. Across from the farm, you'll see the Nacoochee Mound, a burial site used by Native Americans centuries long ago. Self-guided and guided tours are available, outlining the history of the farm and its inhabitants, including the dairy barn's history as the Nacoochee Dairy from 1910 to the mid-1920s.

143 Hwy. 17, Sautee Nacoochee, 706-878-1077
gastateparks.org/HardmanFarm

TIP

Don't miss the Helen to Hardman Heritage Trail, a 1-mile, ADA-accessible trail that connects the Hardman Farm State Historic Site to Helen by following alongside the Chattahoochee River. There are several overlooks as well as interpretive panels regarding native plants and animals.

LEARN ABOUT THE AREA'S NATIVE RESIDENTS
AT THE FUNK HERITAGE CENTER

At the Funk Heritage Center at Reinhardt University in Waleska, visitors can learn about the early Appalachian settlers and Southeastern Indians who made their homes in the North Georgia Mountains. The center offers both guided and self-guided tours. There is a film on the Southeastern Indians that provides background, while the Hall of Ancients features interactive exhibits for more immersive learning. And don't miss the Rogers Contemporary American Indian Art Gallery or the Sellers Collection of Historic Hand Tools, both of which document and provide insight into how these Native Americans and settlers lived. Outside, you can follow the Lou Reeta Barton Northcutt Walking Trail to see the native garden. The Funk Heritage Center provides not only a great introduction to the earliest residents of this area, but also instills an appreciation for how they survived and carried on.

7300 Reinhardt College Cir., Waleska, 770-720-5970
reinhardt.edu/funkheritage

SPEND SOME TIME
AT BOOTH WESTERN ART MUSEUM

Home to the world's largest permanent exhibition space for western art, the Booth Western Art Museum features more than 12 galleries filled with breathtaking paintings, sculptures, photography, and more that showcase the people and land of the American West. One stunning piece is the original 1865 stagecoach in the Neva & Don Rountree Heading West Gallery. An affiliate to the Smithsonian Institution, the museum also includes a Civil War gallery that documents not only major conflicts of the war, but also the struggles of those who took up arms to fight against brothers and neighbors. Another noteworthy space at the Booth is the Carolyn & James Millar Presidential Gallery, which features a portrait and original hand-signed letter from every U.S. president. Encompassing 120,000 square feet, you'll definitely have to return more than once to see and take in all the museum has to offer.

501 Museum Dr., Cartersville, 770-387-1300
boothmuseum.org

TIP
The Booth Museum offers free admission on the first Thursday of every month from 4 to 8 p.m.

FIND OUT ABOUT GEORGIA'S GOLD RUSH
AT THE DAHLONEGA GOLD MUSEUM

Housed in one of Georgia's oldest standing courthouse buildings, the Dahlonega Gold Museum tells the history of the country's first gold rush, which began in the 1820s in Dahlonega. There was so much gold coming out of the mines, a U.S. branch mint opened in 1838. The mint coined more than $6 million in gold before it shut down in 1861. The museum contains a complete set of these coins along with a gold nugget that weighs more than 5 ounces. The museum also honors the building's service as the Lumpkin County Courthouse, including the judge's chambers and the 1889 wooden chapel seats. The Dahlonega Gold Museum periodically hosts special tours that spotlight the building's history, so check the museum's social accounts for upcoming events.

1 Public Square, Dahlonega, 706-864-2257
gastateparks.org/DahlonegaGoldMuseum

DIG FOR FOSSILS
AT THE TELLUS SCIENCE MUSEUM

Located in Cartersville in the foothills of the Appalachian Mountains, the Tellus Science Museum consists of four main galleries with numerous exhibits to help unlock the mysteries of science. In the Weinman Mineral Gallery, you can take a deep dive into Mother Earth and see how it was formed. Two notable exhibits include the periodic table that lights up to show you an example of each element, and the exhibit that shows everyday items that contain various minerals. The Tellus Fossil Gallery showcases fossils from dinosaurs, reptiles, and giant mammals that roamed the earth long, long ago. In the Millar Science in Motion Gallery, examine how technology in transportation has evolved through the years. And in Collins Family My Big Backyard, you'll find interactive exhibits to see how magnets work, thunderstorms develop, and work in an interactive garden. In the Bentley Planetarium, you can explore the solar system and beyond.

100 Tellus Dr., Cartersville, 770-606-5700
tellusmuseum.org

CHECK OUT ARTIST CORNBREAD
AT AROUND BACK AT ROCKY'S PLACE

One of the largest folk-art galleries in the North Georgia Mountains, Around Back at Rocky's Place in Dawsonville showcases thousands of one-of-a-kind art pieces by a wide range of Southern artists, many of whom are self-taught. The gallery's most notable artist is Cornbread, whose real name is John Anderson. A native of Lumpkin County, Cornbread's art focuses on animals that roam local farms and woods, including foxes, quails, guinea hens, deer, turkeys, and others. While Cornbread's chosen medium is painting, you'll also find pottery, woodcarvings, fabric works, and much more by other artists. Visitors to the gallery not only can take in the many artworks, but they also can purchase pieces to take home for their personal collections. When visiting the gallery, be sure to look for an iconic 12-foot-tall blue sculpture, "Our Lady of Dawson," that stands guard by the driveway.

3631 Hwy. 53 E. at Etowah River Rd., Dawsonville, 706-265-6030
aroundbackatrockysplace.com

DIVE INTO CIVIL WAR HISTORY
AT THE CHICKAMAUGA & CHATTANOOGA NATIONAL MILITARY PARK

In 1863, Confederate and Union forces waged battles as each fought to take and retain control of Chattanooga. Control of the city would swing back and forth between both sides before Union troops declared victory in November. At that time, a Confederate soldier wrote, "This . . . is the death-knell of the Confederacy." At the Chickamauga Battlefield Visitor Center, you'll find museum exhibits on the battle of Chickamauga and the campaign for Chattanooga, including the Fuller gun collection. The best place to start is by watching the orientation film so you get the basic back story of the action that took place here. For a more in-depth experience, ranger-led tours are available during the fall and winter months. You also can opt to take a cell-phone tour.

3370 LaFayette Rd., Fort Oglethorpe, 706-866-9241
nps.gov/chch/index.htm

INDULGE YOUR LOVE OF CARS
AT THE SAVOY AUTOMOBILE MUSEUM

A new addition to the North Georgia Mountains, the Savoy Automobile Museum celebrates the automobile in all its glory. From groundbreaking motorcars in the early 1930s to American classics to racecars, and much, much more, the Savoy features some of the most notable cars from the last century. In the Savoy Collection, you'll find vehicles in the museum's permanent collection, although they may rotate periodically to give each car its due. Cars from this collection include a 1932 Buick Model 67, a 1941 Packard 180 LeBaron, and a 1959 Edsel Corsair convertible. Temporary exhibits regularly come and go, but early exhibits included "American Racing," which featured Richard Petty's 1970 Superbird; "Woodies," which highlighted wood-bodied station wagons; and "Orphans," which showcased "lost" automobiles by long-gone car manufacturers. Although the cars on display won't always be the same, one thing will remain: a love for the automobile that transcends time.

3 Savoy Lane, Cartersville, 770-416-1500
savoymuseum.org

TAKE A TOUR
AT THE CHIEF VANN HOUSE

In the 1790s, the Cherokee Indians initiated assimilation efforts to blend in with the American settlers who were taking over their lands. James Vann was a Cherokee Indian leader and wealthy businessman who built up the largest and most prosperous plantation in the Cherokee Nation. Near Chatsworth he built a 2.5-story brick home in 1804, but only lived there a short time before his murder in 1809. His son Joseph carried on his father's success, but as the push to move the Cherokee Nation out continued, the Vann family was forced from their home and sent west on the Trail of Tears. Today, visitors can take a guided tour of this Cherokee Indian home, which features hand carvings, a 12-foot marble mantel, a "floating" staircase, and several antiques. Throughout the year, visitors also can see temporary exhibits such as hand-woven baskets and quilts.

82 Highway 225 N., Chatsworth, 706-695-2598
gastateparks.org/ChiefVannHouse

IMMERSE YOURSELF IN APPALACHIAN HISTORY
AT THE FOXFIRE MUSEUM & HERITAGE CENTER

One of the best ways to learn history is to experience it. At the Foxfire Museum & Heritage Center, visitors can do just that by making their way through the outdoor village that contains more than 20 historic log buildings, each filled with artifacts that represent mountain life from 1820 to 1940. The museum sits on eight acres next to Black Rock Mountain State Park, so it is removed from the usual sights and sounds of modern life, adding to the experience. When going through the buildings, make sure to ring the bell at the chapel. Also, see if you can walk on the stilts at the Shooting Creek cabin. In addition, Foxfire maintains studio space for Appalachian craftsmen and women, so check them out to see such skills as woodworking, weaving, blacksmithing, and more.

98 Foxfire Ln., Mountain City, 706-746-5828
foxfire.org

TIP
Demonstrators operate by their own individual schedule, so call before your visit to find out who will be on-site while you are at Foxfire.

STRIKE IT RICH
AT CONSOLIDATED GOLD MINING CO.

If you've heard of Dahlonega, you've likely heard the town was the site of the original American gold rush. Thousands of miners flocked to the area hoping to strike it rich. At the ground's surface, miners gobbled up the gold, so they implemented new techniques to get more. This led to the formation of the Consolidated Gold Mining Co. Once deep mining was forsaken, the company's mines were abandoned. Then, 75 years later, the mines received new life as a way to hear and learn the history of the gold rush and the miners who sought fortunes. Today, you can travel 200 feet underground during a 40-minute tour for a firsthand look at the difficulties of mining gold from quartz. Following the tour, you'll learn how to pan for gold and get the chance to see if you, too, can strike it rich.

185 Consolidated Gold Mine Rd., Dahlonega, 706-864-8473
consolidatedgoldmine.com

BRING HOME FRUIT-INSPIRED ART
FROM THE GOURD PLACE

Many people think of gourds as a piece of fall décor for their front porch or dining table. But in 1976 Priscilla Wilson started to experiment with gourds as an art medium, creating several pieces that she sold at local craft fairs. The response was favorable, so Wilson kept at it. She also discovered she was far from the only gourd artist out there. Therefore, she and wife Janice Lymburner started collecting gourd art from around the world. In the 1980s, the Gourd Place was born: a museum to display their collection and a shop to sell Wilson's own art, including her Gourd Impressions Pottery, a patented process she created for making pottery with gourd molds. The free museum now houses a permanent collection of more than 200 gourds from 23 countries. Whether you are an art enthusiast, a pottery lover, or neither, this is a destination you can't miss.

2319 Duncan Bridge Rd., Sautee, 706-865-4048
gourdplace.com

PAY HOMAGE TO THE HORSE TROOPER
AT THE 6TH CAVALRY MUSEUM

Opened in 1981, the 6th Cavalry Museum documents the history of the Fighting Sixth Cavalry, which was stationed at The Post at Fort Oglethorpe from 1919 to 1942. However, the 6th Cavalry's story begins much earlier, in 1861, as a U.S. Cavalry regiment. Exhibits in the museum include regimental militaria, weapons, displays about World War II POW camps and the Third Women's Army Corps Training Center, an original Bantam Car (a "jeep"), a tank, and the Shield of Bavaria, the only known official recognition given to an American unit by a German state. The museum sits on the Post's original parade ground and the site is listed on the National Register of Historic Places. Other buildings include 16 original officers' homes, a guardhouse, band barrack, and bandstand.

6 Barnhardt Cir., Fort Oglethorpe, 706-861-2860
6thcavalrymuseum.org

SEE THE STARS
AT THE GEORGE E. COLEMAN SR. PLANETARIUM

Located on the campus of the University of North Georgia in Dahlonega, the George E. Coleman Sr. Planetarium welcomes the public to explore the stars in the night sky. The planetarium features public shows with video on the 30-foot diameter dome combined with a live presentation. These shows change throughout the year, and vary based on the evening skies. You can see everything from stellar nebulas to constellations to the Southern Hemisphere of Earth to various planets in the solar system. Because seating capacity is limited to 46, it's important to book your spot early so you don't miss the shows you want to see. The planetarium schedule is listed and updated on the website. Also open to the public is UNG's North Georgia Astronomical Observatory, complete with a 28-inch reflecting telescope. The observatory's schedule is updated on its Facebook page, so check it out before heading to campus.

**Planetarium: Health and Natural
Sciences Building**
Room 234, 159 Sunset Dr., Dahlonega
706-864-1471
ung.edu/planetarium

Observatory
3000 Dawsonville Hwy., Dahlonega
706-867-2037
facebook.com/UNGObservatory

HONOR OUR VETERANS
AT THE CURRAHEE MILITARY MUSEUM

Housed in the train depot in downtown Toccoa, the Currahee Military Museum shares the stories and history of the World War II paratroopers who trained at Camp Toccoa at Currahee. The soldiers were members of the 501st, 506th, 511th, and 517th Paratrooper Infantry Regiments. These veterans and their families donated most of the artifacts. The museum also features military history for local veterans, the Civil War, and World War I. One unexpected exhibit is a 1922 horse stable that served as housing during World War II in Aldbourne, England. In 2004, it was dismantled and brought to the museum. Before leaving, check out the Stephens County History Museum, also in the train depot. You'll find artifacts, photographs, and exhibits documenting what daily life was like in 1905 and beyond.

160 Alexander St., Toccoa, 706-282-5055
toccoahistory.com

WALK THROUGH A RAILROAD TUNNEL
AT THE TUNNEL HILL
HERITAGE CENTER AND MUSEUM

At the Tunnel Hill Heritage Center and Museum, you will learn how the Western & Atlantic Railroad tunnel was constructed through the Appalachian Mountains and completed in 1850. Measuring 1,477 feet long, the tunnel is quite impressive to behold. It's especially impressive when you learn the Great Locomotive Chase went through the tunnel in April 1862. At first the tunnel looks quite big, but when you see the size of the train that raced through here, it looks much smaller. You can learn about this and other history related to the tunnel and railroad in the museum. When you're ready, you can head out to the tunnel and journey through it. Other stops at the Tunnel Hill Heritage Center and Museum include the Clisby Austin House, which was used as an army field hospital during the Civil War, and the General Store.

215 Clisby Austin Dr., Tunnel Hill, 706-876-1571
civilwarrailroadtunnel.com

NORA MILLS.

NORA
MILLS
EST. 1876
WATER POWERED &
STONE GROUND
CORNMEAL, GRITS,
& WHOLE GRAINS

SORRY - WE ARE
CLOSED

CLOSED

Please place
your order

Photo credit: Len Garrison, Seeing Southern

SHOPPING AND FASHION

ADD TO YOUR OUTDOOR GEAR
AT WANDER NORTH GEORGIA

Who would think starting a blog about their community in the North Georgia Mountains would turn into a highly successful local store filled with apparel, books, artwork, home décor, and more, with many products from local artisans? That's exactly what happened for cofounders Josh and Alex Brown and Jake and Courtney Scott. After relocating to Clayton, the couples and their families met during story time at the local library and just clicked. The Browns already were blogging about life in the North Georgia Mountains, and, after getting to know the Scotts, the four decided to open a storefront in 2016. With inventory driven by what their customers want, it's no surprise locals and visitors flock to Wander North Georgia for their next jacket, a birthday gift, or new travel cups. As part of their commitment to community, the storeowners also donate 1% of their overall sales each month to local Rabun County nonprofits.

87 N. Main St., Clayton, 770-750-4470
wandernorthgeorgia.com

UPDATE YOUR CLOSET OR YOUR HOME
AT ALEXANDER'S

In 1953, Hoyt and Ruby Alexander purchased a small trading post where they sold feed and seed, some groceries, and gas. They soon added a few clothing items and shoes as a result of community need. In 1977, the Alexanders' son Eddy joined the family business, bringing along his own ideas for expansion. He added hardware supplies and appliances as well as guns and ammunition. Eddy's wife, Sandy, then took her turn to grow the business. She expanded the clothing and shoe departments, and, in the mid-1990s, the couple added furniture. Today, Alexander's encompasses 50,000 square feet and serves as the largest department store in the North Georgia Mountains. While it remains a mainstay for locals, it has become a favorite stop for visitors in the area as well. It's a testament to the strength of family-owned and -operated businesses, and solidifies the legacy Hoyt hoped to leave behind.

4482 Town Creek School Rd., Blairsville, 706-745-6450
alexandersstore.com

FIND UNIQUE HOME GOODS
AT GATHER

Located in downtown Blue Ridge, Gather offers a variety of kitchen and home goods, sustainable housekeeping products, specialty treats and items for your pets, and even locally sourced foods and beverages. Wander the sales floor, and you'll see everything from seasonal and holiday décor to dishware to cookbooks to hand soaps and lotions. In the food department, pick your favorites among such items as jams and jellies, small batch popcorn, cookies, specialty drinks, and more. In addition, Gather donates 1% of every purchase to North Georgia charities, with a designated charity chosen each month. So whether you're shopping for something specific or just looking for a new addition to your home, Gather is the perfect spot to pick up something for yourself, a friend, or a loved one.

544 E. Main. St., Blue Ridge, 706-946-1100
gatherblueridge.com

DECORATE YOUR HOME
WITH ARTFUL ELLIJAY
HOME PROVISIONS

Whether you're looking to update your existing décor, decorate a new home, or just want a new piece here and there, Artful Ellijay features a wide range of home goods to fit your needs. Shop for everything from lighting to furniture to wall décor to home accents to seasonal items and much more. The mission is to offer items that are both beautiful and functional so you can create a home you'll love and enjoy. If you need help designing that ideal space, Artful Ellijay's sister store, Artful Provisions Design Center, offers personalized home design services to guide your vision and help turn it into reality. You can visit the design center's showroom to see examples of custom cabinetry, countertops, lighting, flooring, window treatments, paint options, and other home accessories for inspiration and to start planning your own home improvements.

Artful Ellijay Home Provisions
10 N. Main St., Ellijay, 877-244-7755
artfulellijay.com

Artful Provisions Design Center
87 Depot St., Ellijay, 877-244-7755, ext. 3
artfulprovisionsdesigncenter.com

STOCK UP ON FRESH-GROUND CORN AND WHEAT PRODUCTS
AT NORA MILL GRANARY

Built in 1876 by John Martin, Nora Mill has been a mainstay in the North Georgia Mountains, providing fresh-ground corn and wheat for a variety of products. While ownership changed hands through the years, in the early 1980s, retired Army Lt. Col. Ron Fain leased Nora Mill and took over operating the facility, complete with the 1,500-pound French Burr millstones and a 100-foot wooden raceway that sends water to a water turbine. The Fain family continues to manage and operate Nora Mill. As a result, visitors can still purchase ground corn and wheat products such as cornmeal, grits, flours, biscuit and bread mixes, and pancake and waffle mixes. To go with your baked goods, you also can purchase jams, jellies, and syrups, as well as cast-iron cookware, mixing bowls, and other kitchen necessities. It's like bringing home a little part of the North Georgia Mountains.

7107 S. Main St., Helen, 706-878-2375
noramill.com

GO ALL NATURAL
AT FOLK APOTHICS

The roots of Southern Appalachia run deep for many, and that includes Luke and Amanda, owners of Folk Apothics in McCaysville. Not only do they draw from the resources of the land around them, but they also draw upon tried-and-true techniques, recipes, and family traditions to create their many products. The mission is to ensure that approximately 98% of what they sell is made and grown by them. For any items they can't grow or create themselves, they reach out to other local artisans to keep it as homegrown as possible. As a result, you'll find shelves stocked with handmade soaps, mulling spices, teas, washing powders, and more. There's even a selection of mountain medicinals, including salves, bitters, bug spray, and essential oils. If natural is what you want, Folk Apothics just may have it.

2984 Mobile Rd., McCaysville, 706-492-7753
folkapothic.com

STAY IN STYLE
AT JULIANA'S BOUTIQUE

Can you imagine turning a senior capstone project into a thriving retail business? That's exactly how Juliana's Boutique was born. It started as an online venture in 2013, but demand quickly grew for the retailer's fashionable designs. In 2014, Juliana's Boutique opened its first brick-and-mortar store in Blue Ridge, followed soon thereafter by a location in Ellijay. Both stores carry a variety of women's clothing, including dresses, tops, pants, and skirts, as well as shoes and a full range of accessories such as jewelry, hats, belts, handbags, and more. In addition to shopping in-store, you can also still shop online. Merchandise turns over frequently to keep up with changing styles and seasons. Therefore, if you see something you like, you'd better snap it up before it's gone. It's like bringing home a little part of the North Georgia Mountains.

671 E. Main St., Blue Ridge, 706-946-7467

24 S. Main St., Ellijay, 706-276-7467

shopjulianas.com

TAKE YOUR TIME
AT HUCK'S GENERAL STORE

Opened in Blue Ridge in 2008, Huck's General Store carries everything you need or want and everything you didn't know you needed or wanted. You'll find shelves filled with jams, jellies, sauces, butters, sauces, pickles, rubs, and many more food products. And while you're perusing those items, the kids will be trying to decide which of the old-fashioned candy they can talk you into buying. Mary Janes, Chic-O-Sticks, Peanut Butter Bars, and Mini Cow Tales are just a few of the choices, not to mention the licorice, gum, taffy, and other sweet treats. Then there are the hand-cut soaps, books, decorative signs, nostalgic games (jacks, anyone?), T-shirts, and souvenirs. Yes, it's a lot. So when you step through the door, plan to spend more than a few minutes here, lest you miss something you just might have to have. Oh, and don't forget to grab a cold bottled soda before you go!

500 E. Main St., Ste. 201, Blue Ridge, 706-946-4825
hucksgeneralstore.com

CHOOSE A BEAUTIFUL FIGURINE
AT THE GLASSBLOWING SHOP

A mainstay in downtown Helen and Dahlonega, the Glassblowing Shop continues to be a favorite with locals and visitors alike. Opened by flameworkers John and Kathy Warner, the Glassblowing Shop overflows with items created using one of three glass art techniques: flamework glassblowing, furnace working, and stained glass. There are figurines of hummingbirds and flowers, fairies, sea life, musical instruments, and many more. Two popular choices include having your name made in glass and wedding cake toppers. During your visit, take time to watch the Warners' sons, Scott Warner and Chris Kennedy, work on these pieces of art. They regularly host live glassblowing demonstrations to entertain and educate visitors. It's amazing to watch as they create such tiny, intricate pieces of art right there in the store.

8600 Main St., Unit 1, Helen, 706-878-3156

10 S. Chestatee St., Unit F, Dahlonega, 706-864-9022

glassblowingshop.com

ENJOY A TASTE TEST
AT BLUE RIDGE OLIVE OIL COMPANY

Who knew you could—and should—experience a tasting of olive oils? At Blue Ridge Olive Oil Company, which has locations in Blue Ridge and Ellijay, Tom and Donna Harper want customers to not only know and understand the health benefits of olive oil, but also to understand that not all olive oils are alike. They have varied tastes that make one olive oil more suited for a particular dish than another. Pairing those oils with other oils or vinegars adds to the complexities contained within each product. The store carries 65 varieties of olive oil and balsamic vinegars, all of which you can sample. When doing so, make sure you sample the olive oil that tastes great on ice cream. That's right: ice cream.

511 E. Main St., Ste. 100, Blue Ridge, 706-946-6457

24 S. Main St., Ste. F, Ellijay, 706-276-6457

blueridgeoliveoil.com

SCORE A
5¢ CUP OF COFFEE
AT THE DAHLONEGA GENERAL STORE

Right on the square in Dahlonega, the Dahlonega General Store welcomes visitors with the aromas of fresh-brewed coffee and fresh-roasted peanuts. And that coffee? It really is just 5¢ a cup. It's a time-honored tradition that pays homage to days gone by. You'll find other products in the store that also harken back to a previous era, such as nostalgic candy, old-fashioned toys, and Watkins liniment products. The store also carries a line of shirts and hats to commemorate your visit to Dahlonega. Of course, this is just a small sample of the store's inventory. There are history books, home décor, collectibles, food items, nostalgic signs and wall art, knives, moccasins, and more. Yes, you likely will need more than just a few minutes to check out everything available for purchase in the store. That's OK. Take your time, and enjoy a cup of coffee.

24 S. Public Square, Dahlonega, 706-864-2005
dahlonegageneralstore.com

GRAB SOME SNACKS AND SOUVENIRS
AT BETTY'S COUNTRY STORE

Opened in 1973, Betty's Country Store in Helen has been a mainstay for both locals and visitors. Long before Helen was a hot tourist destination, Betty's Country Store was the go-to grocery store for area residents. As more visitors arrived in Helen, they discovered Betty's was the perfect place to grab snacks or buy groceries to cook up in their rental cabin or RV. Today, they still come in to purchase the store's Black Angus beef, fresh cheeses, yogurt-covered pretzels, fresh nuts, and other items. They also make sure they get some of Betty's famous carrot cake and homemade cookies. The store has expanded, now offering imported beer and wine, souvenirs, books, and more. Even if you don't need anything, you can still drop by Betty's Country Store and hang out on the porch, maybe play a game of checkers. Don't worry. There's no rush.

18 Yonah St., Helen, 706-878-2943
facebook.com/BettysCountryStore

STEP BACK IN TIME
AT THE OLD SAUTEE STORE

When you pull up to the Old Sautee Store in Sautee, it looks exactly like what you expect for a store that first opened in 1872: a small, weathered wood building with some rocking chairs on the front porch and Old Glory waving in the breeze. Step through the doors, and your impression won't change much. Along the left are shelves filled with very old foodstuffs, medicines, fabrics, and other items. Walk around, and you'll find shoes and clothes from a bygone era, a fireplace with a mantel clock, carved Indians, and other dated items. It serves as a museum of sorts, preserving a look at life from long ago. Walk through the doorway in the back of the store, though, and you'll step into the present. Racks of apparel, shelves filled with books, candy, art, home décor—it's quite the contradiction. But a great place to grab a souvenir.

2315 Hwy. 17, Sautee, 706-878-2281
sauteestore.com

PICK SOMETHING COOL
AT THE BLAIRSVILLE PICKERS BARN

If you love perusing antique shops, poking behind stacks of old items, or wandering into dusty corners hoping to find a hidden gem, the Blairsville Pickers Barn is for you. This 27,000-square-foot indoor mall includes vendors hawking all kinds of items: jewelry, coins, antiques, knives, furniture, pottery, silver, glassware, handmade items, and a lot more. It's the perfect place to find nostalgic metal signs or pick up seasonal décor or just reminiscence as you walk down the aisles. After all, who doesn't need a traffic light for their basement? Or a stuffed porcupine for the front porch? You might be surprised at what catches your eye as you stroll by. Before you leave, make sure to say hello to Miss Boo, the official mascot for the Blairsville Pickers Barn.

27 Orbit Dr., Blairsville, 706-745-0097
blairsvillepickersbarn.com

GET LOST IN A BOOK
AT BOOK BOUND BOOKSTORE

Independent bookstores are becoming a rarity, making them a precious commodity everywhere, including the North Georgia Mountains. At Book Bound Bookstore in Blairsville, you can still find that sense of community and a deep love of the written word. The store carries books for all ages, and shoppers are encouraged to spend time perusing the shelves for their next purchase. To help build that sense of community, storeowner Sharon Davis also hosts a number of events such as an open poetry night, book clubs, author meet-and-greets, children's story time and other special happenings. She also partners with other local small businesses to further promote community spirit. It's everything independent bookstores are known for, and something we all should strive to keep alive.

35B Blue Ridge St., Blairsville, 706-897-4198
bookboundbooks.com

ACTIVITIES
BY SEASON

WINTER

Adopt a Cabbage Patch Kid at BabyLand General, 92
Pick Something Cool at the Blairsville Pickers Barn, 130
Spend Some Time at Booth Western Art Museum, 99
Find Out About Georgia's Gold Rush at the Dahlonega Gold Museum, 100
Track Down Sasquatch at Expedition Bigfoot, 89
Explore the Impact of Grassroots Art at the Folk Pottery Museum of Northeast Georgia, 88
Learn About the Area's Native Residents at the Funk Heritage Center, 98
Delve Into Racing History at the Georgia Racing Hall of Fame, 91
Dig for Fossils at the Tellus Science Museum, 101
Indulge Your Love of Cars at the Savoy Automobile Museum, 104

SPRING

Take a Tour at the Chief Vann House, 105
Sit In on an Old-Fashioned Appalachian Jam Session, 48
Enjoy the Views From the Etowah Indian Mounds, 90
Find Serenity in Nature at Gibbs Gardens, 65
Step Back in Time at the Hardman Farm State Historic Site, 96
Hike the Appalachian Trail in the North Georgia Mountains, 56
Saddle Up for Some Horseback Riding, 70
Catch Some Baseball With the Rome Braves, 77
Crush Some Cars at Tank Town USA, 60

• •

SUMMER

FALL

SUGGESTED
ITINERARIES

THE GREAT OUTDOORS

GOOD FOR FAMILIES

DIVE INTO HISTORY

GIRLS' WEEKEND

COUPLES' GETAWAY

INDEX